SEEDS OF FRIENDSHIP

To

From

Date

Ribbons of Love™

A Celebration of Sisters

Christmas Wishes From the Heart

Gardens of Friendship

Happy Is the House that Shelters a Friend

Just for You: A Celebration of Joy and Friendship

Loving Thoughts for Tender Hearts

Mother: Another Word for Love

Thoughts From the Garden Gate

Brownlow

SEEDS OF FRIENDSHIP

Edited by Caroline Brownlow · Illustrated by Debbie Mumm

Ever since I could remember anything,

flowers have been like dear friends to me,

comforters, inspirers, powers to uplift and to cheer.

~CELIA THAXTER~

Friends are kind
to each other's dreams.

~Henry David Thoreau~

Who among us has
not sought peace in a song?

~VICTOR HUGO~

One recipe for friendship
is the right mixture
of commonality and
difference. You've got to
have enough in common
so that you understand
each other and enough
difference so that there is
something to exchange.

~Robert Weiss~

All I have seen teaches me
to trust the Creator for
all I have not seen.

~RALPH WALDO EMERSON~

A World Without Flowers

Were the flowers of the world to be taken away, they would leave a blank in creation. Imagination cannot suggest a substitute for them. Whether they flourish in the garden, or bloom in the greenhouse; whether they are scattered in our pathway, sprinkled on the verdant banks, or widely strewn over the hills and vales, they never fail to please; they fill the air with their sweetness; and delight the eye with their beauty.

~Anonymous~

Seed Time

Thine is the seed time:

God alone

Beholds the end of

what is sown;

Beyond our vision

weak and dim

The harvest time

is hid with him.

~JOHN GREENLEAF WHITTIER~

Like life,

few gardens

have only

flowers.

EARLY AMERICAN
PROVERB

Take away love and our earth is a tomb.

~ROBERT BROWNING~

It is bad soil where flowers will not grow.

~EARLY AMERICAN PROVERB~

Kindness in words creates confidence.

Kindness in thinking creates profoundness.

Kindness in giving creates love.

~LAO-TSE~

The good you do is not lost, though you forget it.

~ANONYMOUS~

What sunshine is to flowers,

smiles are to humanity.

~JOSEPH ADDISON~

The highest heavens belong to the Lord,

but the earth he has given to man.

~PSALM 115:16~

It is such a comfort to have a friend near,

When lonesome feelings do come.

~OPAL WHITELEY~

All Things Green

Love of flowers and all things

green and growing is with many women

a passion so strong that it often seems

to be a sort of primal instinct,

coming down through generation

after generation.

~Helena Rutherford Ely~

A Gardener's Education

There is no royal road. It is no use asking me or any one else how to dig—I mean sitting indoors and asking it. Better go and watch a man digging, and then take a spade and try to do it, and go on trying until it comes, and you gain the knack that is to be learnt with all tools, of the doubling of power and halving the effort, and meanwhile you will be learning other things, about your arms and legs and back—and you will find out there are all sorts of ways of learning, not only from people and books, but from sheer trying.

~Gertrude Jekyll~

Greta
The Garden Angel

All nature smiles, and the whole world is pleased.

DAY KELLOGG LEE

To love one's friends, to bathe in life's sunshine, to preserve a right mental attitude— the attitude of gratitude—and to do one's work—these make up an ideal life.

~ELBERT HUBBARD~

Where would we be if humanity
had never known flowers?
If they didn't exist or had always
been hidden from our sight~
would our character, our morals,
our aptitude for beauty, our
happiness be the same?

~MAURICE MAETERLINCK~

The Spirit of Love

You will find, as you look back upon your life, that the moments when you have really lived are the moments when you have done things in the spirit of love.

~HENRY DRUMMOND~

Under the Sun

I will be the gladdest thing
under the sun,
I will touch a hundred
flowers and not pick one.

~EDNA ST. VINCENT MILLAY~

We carry with us
the wonders we seek without us.

~Sir Thomas Browne~

Spring
unlocks
the
flowers
to paint
the
laughing
soil.

~REGINALD HEBER~

Early Morning in the Garden

When in these fresh mornings I go into my garden before anyone is awake, I go for the time being into perfect happiness. In this hour divinely fresh and still, the fair face of every flower salutes me with a silent joy that fills me with infinite content; each gives me its color, its grace, its perfume, and enriches me with the consummation of its beauty.

~Celia Thaxter~

You're supposed to get tired planting bulbs.
But it's an agreeable tiredness.

~GAIL GODWIN~

Every minute, every day, life begins all over again

~ANONYMOUS~

It is not the outside riches but the inside ones
that produce happiness.

~FOLK WISDOM~

I love old gardens best~tired old gardens
that rest in the sun.

~HENRY BELLAMAN~

©Debbie Mumm

Dear friends, let us love one another, for love comes from God. Everyone who loves has been born of God and knows God.

~1 JOHN 4:7~

A Good Turnip Seed

Any one seed may be too old to sprout or inferior in some way, but it will never try to be something it isn't fitted to be. A man may study to be a surgeon when he should have been a shoemaker, a talented painter may spend his life trying to convince himself and his fellows that he is a lawyer, but a turnip seed will never attempt to grow into an ear of corn. If you plant a good turnip seed properly a turnip is what you will get every single time.

~RUTH STOUT~

Everything in life that we really accept
undergoes a change. So suffering must become love.
That is the mystery.

~Katherine Mansfield~

Many eyes go through the meadow,
but few see the flowers.

~Ralph Waldo Emerson~

Let the heavens rejoice, let the earth be glad; let the
fields be jubilant, and everything in them.

~Psalm 96:11,12~

It is only
great souls
that know
how much
glory there
is in
being good.

~SOPHOCLES~

Love Is Not Enough

Love of flowers and vegetables

is not enough to make a good gardener.

He must also hate weeds.

~EUGENE P. BERTIN~

It is not enough to love
those who are near and dear to us.
We must show them that we do so.

~LORD AVEBURY~

Those who
wish to sing always find a song

~Swedish Proverb~

Friend! How sacred the word. Born in the heart of God, and given to man as a treasure from the eternities~no word in the languages so heavily freighted with meaning.

~CYRUS B. NUBBAUM~

Little acts of
kindness which
we render to each
other in everyday life,
are like flowers by the
wayside to the traveler:
they serve to gladden the
heart and relieve the
tandem of life's journey.

~EUNICE BATHRICK~

It Takes Two

The desire for friendship is strong in every human heart. We crave the companionship of those who understand. The nostalgia of life presses, we sigh for "home," and long for the presence of one who sympathizes with our aspirations, comprehends our hopes, and is able to partake of our joys. A thought is not our own until we impart it to another, and the confessional seems to be a crying need of every human soul. One can bear grief, but it takes two to be glad.

~ELBERT HUBBARD~

To dig and delve
in nice clean dirt
can do a mortal
little hurt.

~JOHN KENDRICK BANGS~

Love one

another

deeply

from the

heart

~1 Peter 1:22~

GARDEN

My First Seeds

When I was a little girl, my mother took great pains to interest me in learning to know the birds and wild flowers and in planting a garden. I thought that roots and bulbs and seeds were as wonderful as flowers, and the Latin names on seed packages as full of enchantment as the counting-out rhymes that children chant in the spring. I remember the first time I planted seeds. My mother asked me if I knew the Parable of the Sower. I said I did not, and she took me into the house and read it to me. Once the relation between poetry and the soil is established in the mind, all growing things are endowed with more than material beauty.

~Elizabeth Lawrence~

To stand by the beds at sunrise and
see the flowers awake is a heavenly delight.

~CELIA THAXTER~

If you laugh a lot, when you get older
your wrinkles will be in the right places.

~FOLK WISDOM~

Life begets life. Energy creates energy.
It is by spending oneself that one becomes rich.

~SARAH BERNHARDT~

The cure for all the ills and wrongs, the cares, the sorrows, and the crimes of humanity, all lie in the one word "love." It is the divine vitality that everywhere produces and restores life.

~LYDIA MARIA CHILD~

A Garden Doorway

To me, the garden is a doorway to other worlds; one of them, of course, is the world of birds. The garden is their dinner table, bursting with bugs and worms and succulent berries (so plant more to accommodate you both).

~ANNE RAVER~

Greta
The Garden Angel

Friendship
is a plant
which
must
often be
watered.

GERMAN PROVERB

Seasoned Words

Let my

words be

sweet and

good, for

tomorrow

I may have

to eat them.

~FOLK WISDOM~

The beautiful is as useful as
the useful, perhaps more so.

~VICTOR HUGO~

All are needed by each one;
Nothing is fair or good alone.

~RALPH WALDO EMERSON~

'Tis always morning somewhere.

~HENRY WADSWORTH LONGFELLOW~

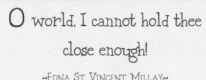

O world, I cannot hold thee
close enough!
~Edna St. Vincent Millay~

A great deal of what we see still
depends on what we're looking for.
~Anonymous~

Everything we do, dear friends,
is for your strengthening.
~2 Corinthians 12:19~

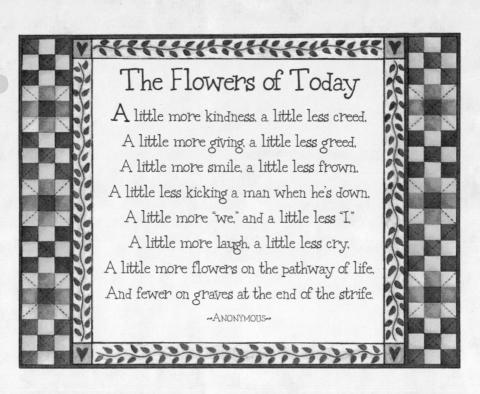

The Flowers of Today

A little more kindness, a little less creed,

A little more giving, a little less greed,

A little more smile, a little less frown,

A little less kicking a man when he's down,

A little more "we," and a little less "I,"

A little more laugh, a little less cry,

A little more flowers on the pathway of life,

And fewer on graves at the end of the strife.

~Anonymous~

Beauty and Joy Were There

I am in love with this world. I have climbed its

mountains, roamed its forests, sailed its waters,

crossed its deserts, felt the sting of its frosts, the

oppression of its heats, the drench of its rains,

the fury of its winds, and always have beauty

and joy waited upon my goings and comings.

~JOHN BURROUGHS~

As you sow,
so shall ye
reap~unless
of course
you are an
amateur
gardener.

~ANONYMOUS~

The Power of Love

Often I hear people say, "How do you make your plants flourish like this?" as they admire the little flower patch I cultivate in summer, or the window gardens that bloom for me in the winter; "I can never make my plants blossom like this! What is your secret?" And I answer with one word, "Love." For that includes all,—the patience that endures continual trial, the constancy that makes perseverance possible, the power of foregoing ease of mind and body to minister to the necessities of the thing beloved, and the subtle bond of sympathy which is as important, if not more so, than all the rest.

CELIA THAXTER

If you haven't forgiven yourself something,
how can you forgive others?

~Dolores Huerta~

The would-be gardener requires
more patience than most mortals!

~Celia Thaxter~

The Infinite has written its name
on the heavens in shining stars,
and on the earth in tender flowers.

~Jean Paul Richter~

SUNFLOWER
SEEDS

©Debbie Mumm

We've been
friends so long
that we're
beginning to look
like each other.

~ANONYMOUS~

GOOD
FRIENDS

©Debbie Mumm

It is only by doing the common things uncommonly well, doing them with pride and enthusiasm, and just as well, as neatly, as quickly, and as efficiently as possible, that you take the drudgery out of them. This is what counts in the final issue. How can you expect to do a great thing well when you half do the little things? These are the stepping-stones to the great things.

~Orison Swett Marden~

Those who give love,
gather love.

~ANONYMOUS~

A Time for Each

Nothing is a better lesson in the knowl-
edge of plants than to sit down in front
of them, and handle them and look them
over just as carefully as possible and
giving plenty of time to each kind of little
plant, examining it closely and asking
oneself, and it, why this and why that.

~Gertrude Jekyll~

Serving

God is

doing good

to man.

BENJAMIN FRANKLIN

Don't refuse to go on an occasional wild goose chase;
that is what wild geese are made for.

~Henry S. Haskins~

It probably would be all right if we'd love
our neighbors as we love ourselves, but could
they stand that much affection?

~Anonymous~

There is a miracle in every new beginning.

~Herman Hesse~

The best way to be understood is to be understanding.

~Anonymous~

Love and the gentle heart
are but a single thing.

~Dante Alighieri~

A Little Flower

Thanks to the human heart by which we live,

Thanks to its tenderness, its joys and fears,

To me the meanest flower that blows can give

Thoughts that do often lie too deep for tears.

~William Wordsworth~

Sunshine for the Soul

Flowers always make people better, happier, and more helpful; they are sunshine, food and medicine to the soul.

~Luther Burbank~

He that plants trees

loves others besides himself.

~THOMAS FULLER~

The Mystery of Life

Working in the garden gives me a profound feeling of inner peace. Nothing here is in a hurry. There is no rush toward accomplishment, no blowing of trumpets. Here is the great mystery of life and growth. Everything is changing, growing, aiming at something, but silently, unboastfully, taking its time.

~RUTH STOUT~

Wayside Sacraments

Never lose an opportunity of
seeing anything that is beautiful;
for beauty is God's handwriting~a
wayside sacrament. Welcome it in
every fair face, in every fair sky,
in every fair flower, and thank
God for it as a cup of blessing.

~RALPH WALDO EMERSON~

One of the
healthiest
ways to
gamble is with
a spade and a
package of
garden seeds.

~Dan Bennett~

More important than length of life
is how we spend each day.

~MARIA A. FURTADO~

All gardens are a form of autobiography.

~ROBERT DASH~

Exclusiveness in a garden is a mistake
as great as it is in society.

~ALFRED AUSTIN~

It is almost impossible to smile on the outside
without feeling better on the inside.

~ANONYMOUS~

There is one thing that you will find
practically impossible to carry into your
own greenhouse and that is tension.

~CHARLES H. POTTER~

The great tragedy of life is not that men perish,
but that they cease to love.

~SOMERSET MAUGHAM~

Give what you have. To someone it may
be better than you dare to think.

~HENRY WADSWORTH LONGFELLOW~

The Lessons of a Garden

But a garden is at once the most delightful and cunning of teachers. How kindly are the virtues it inculcates!~ Patience, faith, hope, tenderness, gratitude, resignation, things in themselves as fragrant and beautiful as the flowers, or like the herbs, a little repellent of aspect, but sweet in their bruised savor.

~AGNES AND EGERTON CASTLE~

A Seed Once Sown

The lesson I have thoroughly learnt, and wish to
pass on to others, is to know the enduring happiness
that the love of a garden gives. I rejoice when I see
anyone, and especially children, inquiring about
flowers, and wanting gardens of their own, and care~
fully working in them. For love of gardening is
a seed that once sown never dies, but always grows
and grows to an enduring and
ever~increasing source of happiness.

~GERTRUDE JEKYLL~

Greta
The Garden Angel

What is a friend? A single soul dwelling in two bodies.

ARISTOTLE

Hoe while it is spring, and enjoy the best anticipations. It is not much matter if things do not turn out well.

CHARLES DUDLEY WARNER

Those who have the largest hearts have the soundest understandings; and he is the truest philosopher who can forget himself.

~WILLIAM HAZLITT~

When we forget ourselves, we usually do something that everyone else remembers.

~ANONYMOUS~

If we learn how to give ourselves, to forgive others, and to live with thanksgiving, we need not seek happiness~it will seek us.

~JOSEPH FORT NEWTON~

Places to Play,
Places to Pray

Everybody needs beauty as
well as bread, places to play
in and pray in, where Nature
may heal and cheer and give
strength to body and soul alike.

~JOHN MUIR~

Laws of Nature

There is a wonderful, mystical law of nature that the three things we crave most in life—happiness, freedom, and peace of mind—are always attained by giving them to someone else.

—UNKNOWN—

Gardening is an exercise in optimism. Sometimes it is the triumph of hope over experience.

~Marina Schinz~

Our happiness is greatest when we contribute most to the happiness of others.

FOLK WISDOM